FOCUS ON THE FAMILY ®

HELP!
SOMEONE I KNOW HAS A PROBLEM WITH PORN

HELP!
SOMEONE I KNOW HAS A PROBLEM WITH PORN

dr. bill maier
general editor

jim vigorito, ph.d.
author

Tyndale House Publishers, Inc.
Carol Stream, Illinois

A Focus on the Family book published by
Tyndale House Publishers, Carol Stream, Illinois 60188

TYNDALE and Tyndale's quill logo are registered trademarks of Tyndale House
Publishers, Inc.

Editor: Brandy Bruce
Cover photograph © by Laurence Dutton/Getty Images. All rights reserved.

Library of Congress Cataloging-in-Publication Data
Maier, Bill.
  Help! : someone I know has a problem with porn / Bill Maier, Jim Vigorito.
— 1st ed.
      p. cm. — (Help! series)
  ISBN-13: 978-1-58997-175-2
  ISBN-10: 1-58997-175-2
  1. Pornography. 2. Sex addiction. 3. Sex addicts—Rehabilitation. I. Vigorito,
Jim, 1949- II. Title. III. Series: Help! (Carol Stream, Ill.)
  HQ471.M315 2006
  241'.667—dc22
                                          2006012790

Printed in the United States of America
1 2 3 4 5 6 7 8 9 / 11 10 09 08 07 06

Contents

Foreword

. . . porn is now virtually everywhere. The users are no longer just fraternity boys and those written off as "dirty old men." Now, the users of virtually unrestricted porn include children, teenagers, and adults of all ages. The victims include not only those whose lives, marriages, relationships, careers, and sexuality are corrupted, but also everyone involved in the vast pornography industry at every stage.[1]

These words clearly illustrate that America has a major problem with pornography. In fact, industry statistics indicate that 70 percent of 18- to 24-year-old men visit pornographic websites in a typical month. Of men in their twenties and thirties, 66 percent report that they are regular users of porn.[2]

No doubt you've picked up this book because you or someone you love is addicted to viewing pornography. You may be emotionally devastated because you recently discovered that your spouse has been living a "secret life" involving internet pornography. Perhaps you are personally struggling with a pornography addiction—you've been plagued by guilt and shame and you've finally decided to get help.

In this book, my colleague Jim Vigorito will help you tackle this issue head-on. Jim will educate you, challenge you, and come alongside you as a trusted friend and counselor. He'll provide you with the practical steps you need to take to help your loved one—or help yourself.

I pray that God will use this resource to start you and your family down a path toward healing and wholeness!

Dr. Bill Maier
Vice President, Psychologist in Residence
Focus on the Family

Introduction

Sonia's Story

Sonia was sobbing so hard that she could not speak. Amid pauses where she attempted to catch her breath, she told the counselor that she had just found hundreds of nude pictures saved on her husband's computer. She felt completely betrayed by his behavior. How could he take sexual pleasure from an on-screen image while she lay exhausted from a day of caring for two children? On their wedding day, this man had promised to remain faithful to her alone. She was conflicted between her disgust at what he had done and her concern for the person she loved.

9 9 9

Lucy's Story

Lucy couldn't believe that her well-behaved 11-year-old son was looking at images of men having sex with one another. His eyes welled up with tears when she confronted him. He said that one day he and a friend were looking up different Web sites when suddenly a picture of two men kissing came onto the screen. They giggled at first and then tried to exit the site. But new and more-disturbing images came up. They didn't tell anyone because they were afraid of getting into trouble. It wasn't long before they were going back to the computer to see if they could sneak a peek at some new pictures. He told Lucy he knew that what he had been doing was wrong, and that he really wanted to stop. He just didn't know how.

ᘎ ᘎ ᘎ

Jose's Story

Jose was shocked when Mike, a coworker and close friend, admitted to him that he had struggled with an attraction to pictures of young girls for many years. The problem started when a friend dared her younger sister to lift her shirt in front of him. Ever since that time, he was drawn to look at pictures of topless preteen girls. Mike didn't think that his porn addiction was a big deal. Jose knew he needed more information before he could confront Mike about the seriousness of porn addiction and offer him the help and support he needed.

ဝ ဝ ဝ

Sonia, Lucy, and Jose represent a growing number of people who know someone with a problem with pornography. It has been estimated that the annual revenue of the U.S. porn industry exceeds $10 billion.

And some surveys show that up to 40 million Americans regularly view Internet pornography.[3] These statistics indicate that the chances are good someone you know has a problem with pornography. Maybe your situation is similar to Sonia's—you've discovered that your spouse has viewed pornography online. Or perhaps you've caught another family member in the act. It's possible that you suspect someone you know of having a porn addiction, but you're not sure.

Don't be deceived by cultural misconceptions; pornography use is wrong and not only harms the user, but also his or her family. By picking up this book, you have chosen to take the first step in helping your loved one or friend. This book is designed to offer practical advice by defining pornography, diagnosing the problem, and offering the hope of solutions.

Part
One

Defining
Pornography

The word *pornography* is defined in Webster's as "The depiction of erotic behavior (as in pictures or writing) intended to cause sexual excitment." Our word *prostitute* comes from the same Greek root (*porne*). As with a prostitute, the customer viewing pornography pays for sexual arousal apart from any relationship. The sexual desire is entirely fantasy driven, with no connection to real life. It is completely self-preoccupied. The customer determines the content and the timing. Apart from payment, nothing else is either given by or expected from the customer.

Different Outlets of Pornography

Access to pornography has changed dramatically in the past two decades. Magazines, books, and later, films were the primary vehicles of sale in the previous

century. The euphemisms "adult" or
"mature" were used to denote themes that
society viewed as inappropriate for minors.
Apart from mail-order deliveries of pornographic material arriving at the door in
brown paper, porn customers ran the risk
of personal exposure in pursuit of these
items.

The advent of the Internet has brought
at least five major changes to the pornography industry:

- Increased accessibility
- Interactive capability
- Dramatic lowering of the age of first
  exposure
- Expansion of offerings
- Entrée to personal encounters

Pornography is now *instantly acces-
sible* in the home. Unsolicited pop-ups can
appear when you make a slight typing
error. Images and videos can be down-

loaded without risk of outside exposure. Many of these materials can be obtained and utilized without the knowledge of parents or spouses. Technology permitting downloading to cell phones and other handheld devices means potential access to pornography anywhere and at any time.

Beyond increased accessibility, the Internet has *interactive capability*, which permits exchange of conversation and personal images in a way that was hardly imaginable a short time ago. Through chat rooms and video exchange, participants explore sexual fantasy from the privacy of their homes. Because people from all over the world can be signed on, locating someone interested in sex is never a problem. Previous limitations of geographical location and after-hours availability are a thing of the past.

It also appears that the Internet has *dramatically lowered the age of first exposure* to pornography. The young, the curious, and the inexperienced were, and still are, the most vulnerable customers. While there were always exceptions, pornography use tended to peak in adolescence and early adulthood. Pornography access for young children was limited to materials left around by parents or other elders. Focus on the Family now receives a number of calls from parents of preteens, such as Lucy. Their children have access to and are compulsively viewing pornography before even reaching puberty. In many cases, their Internet access has not been supervised closely enough.

Internet access has also resulted in an *expansion of offerings* in pornography. Having worked in the rehabilitation of sexual offenders for more than 25 years, I

used to think that I had heard it all. But
with its worldwide clientele, the Internet
now makes it profitable to cater to very
specific and ever-changing sexual tastes.
Web sites and chat groups pander to an
endless variety of sexual preferences that
run the gamut from sadomasochism to
dressing as infants.

As serious as the first four changes are,
the entrée to personal encounters represents
the greatest safety risk for porn users of
any age. Pornography has always served as
an entryway to greater sexual deviance and
potential harm. The impression is given
that the inevitable next step after porn use
is personal physical involvement. And
unlike infamous porn stars of the past
(many of whom were forced to perform out
of drug dependency and worse), present-
day online participants may wish to be
contacted. The next step in their virtual

sexual exchange is a real-life meeting with someone they know almost nothing about.

Despite countless newspaper accounts of the risk of murder and sexual assault, husbands, fathers, wives, and mothers suddenly disappear, taking the family savings or a credit card to finance a cross-country rendezvous. Children and teens also fall into this trap, leaving home to meet strangers, ignoring the danger. They may not know the person's real identity, let alone previous criminal activities or presence of sexually transmitted diseases. A 16-year-old girl may think she's going to see a boy her age, only to meet a middle-aged sex offender.

Gender Differences in Pornography Usage

Not that long ago, viewing pornography magazines was primarily a male thing.

Many in society accepted the practice as a male rite of passage. Over time, the women models wore less, and the poses became more explicit and provocative. The women were treated as objects at best, and sex was always portrayed as an activity devoid of commitment or self-sacrifice.

Once initiated into the world of pornography, many men found that magazines did not compare to live action. Adult films left nothing to the imagination. It was not unusual for my male counseling clients to talk about following particular female porn stars throughout a series of films. The men were attracted to these women on the basis of a particular hair color, height, or specific body build. It was as if the criteria of attractiveness involved a set of visual templates. The objects of their attraction were two-dimensional cutouts bearing no resemblance to flesh-and-blood personalities.

Men in particular have a capacity to *compartmentalize*. They view their lives in separate compartments rather than as a consistent whole. On Sunday mornings, they enter the church compartment. On Tuesday evenings, while their wives are at aerobics class or choir practice, they enter the "little something for me" compart-ment. They don't see the bearing one has upon the other. Those who use pornogra-phy on occasion may fail to appreciate the extent to which it can totally disrupt their lives and the lives of others. But the more one engages in the activity, the greater the likelihood that it will consume one's thoughts.

In the past, women were drawn mostly to steamy romance novels. Instead of playing the visual card, women chose a relational alternative. In greatest demand were men who listened, sacrificed, and catered to their every wish. *Rich* didn't hurt, but conversationalists able to appreciate more than just physical beauty were highly sought after. At the time, it seemed harmless to leave the demands of daily routine for just a little escape and a sense of appreciation.

Chat rooms have drastically changed the pornography playing field for both men and women. Men who barely speak in the home stay up all night chatting with their newly-found soul mates. Women who are discreet in dealing with men at church or in the workplace let down their guard in the anonymity of their home computer. Internet games and chat rooms provide the illusion of security. Fantasy role-play provides the opportunity to try a different personality without the commitment of an ongoing relationship.

Pornography's Damage to the Family

The first obvious danger of porn is the time it takes away from important responsibilities. Not only does viewing pornography take time away from family and friends, but in some cases pornography has also overtaken users' lives—even causing men and women to lose their jobs. A growing number of men and women are accessing Internet pornography while at work.

As with any addiction, the compulsion grows as the habit is fed. The desire for more outweighs the importance of other duties. For example, a man can't give his very best at his job for eight hours, come home and willingly help his wife with dinner, share in the burden of bathing and settling in the children, engage in meaningful conversation with his wife— and then have reserve energy to stay on the computer all night chatting with a woman he's never met. If he *is* choosing to spend hours on the computer at night, other responsibilities are suffering. For one thing, the relationship with his spouse is being neglected.

Disruption in the relationship with one's spouse hurts the children, too. When there is instability in the marital relationship, spouses often withdraw from each other out of fear of being hurt by the other. But by withdrawing, both spouses also become less engaged emotionally in meeting the needs of their children.

A third danger posed by porn is the tendency to create unrealistic expectations of the opposite sex. The "centerfold syndrome" takes its name from pornography magazines that highlight a colorful two-page stapled photo of someone new each month. The phrase refers to the problem of how pornography affects the way men view women and sex. This syndrome creates a false standard that is impossible for either partner or spouse to attain. Computer enhancement eliminates flab, hides blemishes, and augments curves. The promise that next month will bring a more tantalizing centerfold implies that others are disposable objects useful only to the extent that they satisfy the viewer's urges in the present.

No wife can compete with the centerfold image. Unlike a photograph, real-life blemishes aren't so easily covered. Additionally, false comparisons are created to ideal images that a real-life person can never match. Pornography creates misconceptions by devaluing women and men to the extent that only the outside image matters.

Furthermore, the centerfold syndrome leads men to think of women—including their wives—as nothing more than sexual objects who exist only to fulfill their every fantasy. This distorted view and the expectations that go with it become a cancer that can easily destroy a marriage.

The counterpart to the centerfold syndrome for women is the romantic ideal of "Mr. Wonderful." More important than possessing washboard abs and sculptured facial features, this highly sensitive male sacrificially places his mate's emotional needs before everything else. He is decisive, yet tender. He values who she is on the inside and doesn't merely regard her as a pretty face. He would never put the demands of his job ahead of catering to her. In both cases, pornography distorts reality, causing both men and women to find dissatisfaction in the reality of their lives.

Another danger of pornography is the potential for long-term behavioral problems. Secular culture has concluded that some sexual outlet should be provided for those who are not married. One difficulty with this belief is that the habit of arousing sexual passion before marriage, whether by visual image or romanticized relationship, often persists into marriage. The strength of the fantasy attraction, repeated over the years, may well be stronger than the real-life sexual experience of husband and wife. How can this be? The fantasy relationship often preceded the real relationship. Years of repeated behavior created a preferred method of pleasure that seemed natural and easy. Breaking this behavioral pattern is difficult and takes time and effort.

Pornography use (whether preceding or coinciding with the marriage) also violates the wedding vow to be sexually faithful to one's spouse; it therefore breaks the bond of trust. When that infidelity is exposed, family members who are hurt by the betrayal must work to find healing also.

Another serious danger is the fact that engaging in pornography puts other family members at risk for the same behavior. Occasionally, a person will report that curiosity about the hold pornography had on the spouse led to his or her own entrapment. The careful removal of physical evidence of pornography does not eliminate the risk to the family. Many children and teens have been exposed to pornography by discovering materials their parents have used. Frances graphically illustrated this point in a recent letter to Focus on the Family:

My heart was broken today when I found my 10-year-old son looking at Internet pornography. His father also had a problem with pornography, which played a large role in the dissolution of our marriage. Fortunately, he has since gotten help and has joined me in talking to our son.

This topic disturbs me because I personally know the damage caused by viewing pornography. You see, my stepfather left pornographic magazines out for me to see. I never felt that I could measure up to the images in those magazines. I went through a period of promiscuity before getting married.

The nature of pornography is such that the user often becomes desensitized to the explicit images he has viewed and then escalates to more graphic and disturbing images. Even worse, porn addiction often leads to progressively worse behaviors, such as going to strip clubs and hiring prostitutes. In extreme cases, porn addiction has resulted in rape and physical abuse; the user begins acting out certain deviant fantasies. As stated earlier, the Internet provides an outlet for not only pornographic images but also the potential to meet strangers with the same interests and addictions.

But regardless of the level of pornography being viewed, using it is unhealthy and hurts the user and his or her family.

Beware of Bad Advice

Our culture offers many false assurances that looking at pornography is no big deal. Older men may smile as they recall having looked at magazines or viewed adult videos in their teens. They do not see the harm in the behavior because they may not have experienced the full destructiveness of the activity. I am concerned that today's greater accessibility to porn, the availability of more brazen images, and the potential to have personal interaction increase the chances that the problem will be more difficult to shake.

Others in our culture may excuse the behavior because they still struggle with pornography themselves. They do not recognize the extent of their problem, nor the harm it is doing in their own lives. Some addicts refuse to stop looking at

porn, insisting that there's nothing wrong
with it, and look for ways to justify their
actions. A recent letter to Focus on the
Family from a military wife illustrates this
problem of acceptance of pornography:

> I think you should know the seri-
> ousness of pornography in our mil-
> itary now. . . . On submarines there
> is hardcore porn everywhere . . .
> the head, on the tables, and in the
> "community lockers." . . . They are
> playing porn on their computers
> and the televisions in the common
> areas. Many of the chaplains
> excuse the behavior because they
> use pornography themselves.

The consequences of accepting
pornography as "normal" are staggering.
Many who struggle with pornography

stop trying to overcome it when they hear authorities labeling the behavior as normal. Some will strike out at spouses: "See, I told you that you were making a big deal about nothing!"

Spouses are sometimes told that *they* are responsible for the partner's looking elsewhere. Even pastors and close friends may say that it is the fault of the spouse for not meeting the partner's sexual needs. ***Pornography use is never the spouse's fault!*** Besides, in most cases, the perceived sexual "needs" are unrealistic.

Pornography use, followed by masturbation, has created an insatiable monster. Some people with this problem demand to have sexual relations on a daily basis. They insist upon having sex after ignoring the spouse, or even being verbally or physically abusive. They may demand sexual practices that the spouse finds unpleasant or even painful.

Perhaps added to this humiliation is the charge that the spouse has failed to maintain sexual attractiveness or enthusiasm. The spouse is told, "It's no wonder I looked elsewhere." Already struggling from the blow of personal betrayal, the spouse now reels under the finger of blame and false guilt.

Of course, the sexual relationship between a husband and wife is a two-way street. Both spouses share in the responsibility for maintaining communication and creating times for intimacy. However, turning to pornography is never a legitimate part of relational healing. Because it represents a distortion of the sexual gift, no good can come from it. It drives a wedge between spouses rather than fostering the unity and oneness that are ultimately desired.

Part
Two

Understanding
Addiction

Psychologist Dr. Archibald Hart suggests that pornography use has both *addictive* and *compulsive* motivational components.[4] *Addictions* are repetitive behaviors whose main attraction is pleasurable benefit. *Compulsions* are repetitive behaviors whose main attraction is relief from painful emotions.

On the addictive side, people are drawn to the pleasurable experience of arousal and sexual release. They want more experiences comparable to the last one. Because the body also adapts to stimulation, just a little more stimulus is required to produce the same effect the next time. This process is called *progression*. Taken together, the addictive and progressive properties demand more and varied experiences to produce the desired positive effect.

On the compulsive side, one seeks out

sexual arousal to cope with deep emotional pain. Sexual abuse, particularly when perpetrated by a family member or other trusted authority, qualifies as a major source of deep emotional pain. A sexual response can become the comfort of choice. Unresolved emotional pain can be triggered by new experiences of rejection, or just resurface spontaneously. The mechanism of *progression* also applies to the compulsive motivation. New and varied sexual stimuli may be necessary to produce the accustomed level of sexual comfort.

From an addictive perspective, people become stuck (or fixated) at the place "where the addiction takes over." In other words, there comes a time when the addicted person stops growing cognitively, emotionally, and socially. For example, despite being in his early forties,

Jonathan talked like a teen, wore his hair like a teen, and still socialized like a teen. His appearance matured only after he made progress in treatment.

How this mechanism operates is not fully clear, but it may be that when a certain percentage of energy is directed toward a solitary pursuit, there is not enough energy left to constructively engage in other areas of development. In adult alcoholics, for example, attaining sobriety is only the beginning of recovery. A major part of addiction recovery work involves returning to the point of fixation and training the person how to think, feel, and relate. The person needs to develop reasoning and relational skills that either were never learned, or were never utilized, during the teen and adult years.

From a compulsive perspective,

trauma keeps people from properly processing subsequent events. Normally, people process events simultaneously along
many different dimensions, among which
are thoughts, feelings, and the five senses
(sight, sound, smell, touch, and taste).
We process the moment, and then move
on to face what comes next. Some believe
that trauma causes processing overload.
Situations that resemble the original
trauma may unexpectedly trigger the
original overwhelming emotions. A reser-
voir of pain and confusion lies just
beneath the surface. It can be triggered at
any time.

Family and friends walk on eggshells
because they are never really sure what
will trigger a person's access to the reser-
voir of old pain. Many clinicians believe it
is necessary to return to the original
trauma to help the individual properly

process that event in all its dimensions. Once this processing occurs, later life events may also have to be reprocessed. Like a zipper that has gotten off track, all subsequent processing is off track. Eduardo is an example:

Eduardo was treated harshly by his parents. His father would strike him repeatedly for minor offenses—a never-ending series of small traumas, if you will. He believed there was nothing he could do to earn his father's approval. Life for Eduardo was unpredictable and terrifying.

The summer before he began second grade, Eduardo was surprised when an older neighbor invited him over to his house to play. Eduardo was on cloud nine. Finally he felt noticed and appreciated! After some time,

Eduardo was shown pornographic magazines belonging to the friend's father. Eduardo sensed that there was something wrong with looking at these magazines, but nothing else felt safe in his life. From that time on in Eduardo's life, when he felt afraid, lonely, or inadequate—those feelings instilled in him by an abusive father—he looked to pornography as a safe retreat. Pornography became a compulsive addiction for Eduardo, because he repeatedly turned to it for comfort and safety.

Processing overload can be positively terrifying. The inability to process emotional stimuli can produce profound confusion. A person may not know who she is, where she is, or what is going on. In this state of total panic, people reach for something familiar to ground them in reality. If sexual pleasure brings some relief, it is sought the next time chaos knocks at the door. For the addict, it is beyond comprehension to give up the one place he or she goes when hurting.

Part Three

Diagnosing
the Issue

Overcoming denial is the first hurdle to diagnosing the issue of porn addiction. Denial is the buffer between reality and the ability to personally process it. Denial says, "I'm not ready to deal with the facts just yet. Come back later." In healthy individuals, denial gradually gives way to acceptance of the facts.

Approaching others with the message that there is something wrong with the way they pursue sex is likely to be met with denial or other forms of resistance. The more developed the problem is, the greater the intensity of the reaction. For some men or women tangled up in the web of pornography, the belief that this kind of sexual gratification is the most important thing in their lives has taken over. They cannot imagine living life any other way.

Defensiveness is the second struggle in

diagnosing porn addiction. Defensiveness is an interesting phenomenon. If you
were to accuse me of having embezzled a
million dollars, I would laugh out loud.
The charge couldn't possibly stick because
there isn't a shred of evidence to support
it. My home, the car I drive, the clothes I
wear, my bank account, and my spending
habits show no evidence of large sums of
money having ever been present. There is
no need for me to be defensive in the
least.

On the other hand, I will become
defensive when you suggest that I am
messy. I immediately begin making
excuses that I have too many projects
going on at once. I'll also throw in a little
blame: "Everyone expects me to keep
track of everything." All of this is said in
defense of a habit for which I am embar-

rassed. I say that my messiness doesn't bother me that much, but it does. I'm just a little overwhelmed with what it will take to change such a long-standing habit.

At some level, most people struggling with pornography know there is a problem. Despite dogged pursuit, this kind of sex fails to fully satisfy. Addiction and compulsion have in common the false belief that sexual release will fix everything. The reality is that sex will *not* fix everything. Denial and defensiveness are symptoms of a deeper problem. Understanding, and then correcting, the deeper issue is intimidating for at least two reasons:

First, people who struggle with pornography have often made efforts to overcome the attraction on their own—and failed. They are likely to be frustrated, and may have concluded (albeit falsely) that they are beyond help.

Second, shame is frequently connected with pornography use. Most pornography users are constantly vigilant for fear of detection. Secrecy is maintained as protection from rejection.

Yet, the problem must be faced head on if a pornography addiction is ever going to be overcome. Denial and defensiveness are two major indicators that someone has a problem he or she is not yet ready to deal with, but what are some other signs that someone may have a problem? Below are a few warning signs that someone may be struggling with a porn addiction:

- Withdrawing from intimacy
- Isolating within the home
- Missing family activities
- Staying up past usual bedtime

- Secrecy about activities (especially computer use)
- Blaming others when confronted

Keep in mind that showing one or more of these behaviors does not necessarily mean that your loved one has a porn addiction; however, if you notice a negative change in behavior patterns, talk about it with that person. Let him know that you've noticed the change and give him an opportunity to talk about the problem.

Overcoming Denial

In 25 years of counseling experience, I've learned that people can be quite good at hiding the truth from themselves and others. Even experienced therapists can have trouble discovering the underlying truth. It shouldn't come as a surprise when family and friends who *want* to believe in the truthfulness of their loved one also over-look the obvious warning signs.

People hide from the truth for many reasons. Disclosure may result in dire consequences, such as an ultimatum to stop or to move out of the home. Disclo-sure risks an end to an activity that is pleasurable.

It is often necessary to uncover think-ing errors that may have little to do with sex. Examples of thinking errors include *entitlement* (I deserve the best things without having to make a persistent effort) and *exception* (the general rules do not apply to me). Men will go to great lengths to protect their unhealthy behavior, often resorting to other forms of deception. Some maintain sterling reputations in other aspects of their lives. Who would ever suspect such an upstanding person of having a darker side?

Women also cover their tracks. To avoid suspicion, some women will overdo their attentiveness to the home or the children. They may say they are spending time with a girlfriend, when in reality they are developing a relationship with another man.

Twisting the truth runs the continuum from outright lying, to omitting incriminating details, to deliberately misleading others into drawing false conclusions. On the next level of truth twisting are the excuses made for such behavior, such as minimizing and blaming: "It only happens once in a while." "Everybody does it." "If you would only give me what I need."

Unspeakable shame and fear of further rejection drive the sexual behavior to secrecy. Unwittingly, the secrecy adds fuel to the compulsion by deepening the sense of isolation. Beneath this fear is the belief that if others really knew what was going on, they would totally reject the person.

We often hear the complaint from loved ones, "I just wish (s)he would admit that (s)he's got a problem." Sadly, the person with the pornography problem is often the last one to see the full extent of it. It is very frustrating for the spouse to feel like his or her life is on hold until the addict makes a decision. This frustration may lead to intense anger, feelings of helplessness, or even depression. But bringing the matter of another's sexual problem to light, though unpleasant, is often necessary.

Scripture is clear about the importance of first dealing with one's own heart before tackling the correction of another.[5] This caution doesn't mean that only the sinless may speak. In that case, we would all keep silent. But the likelihood of our being heard is increased when we approach the person who is struggling with a heart of compassion, rather than one of judgment.

A story is told of a man who had four sons. He wanted his sons to learn not to judge things too quickly. He sent out each of the sons independently to look for, and then to report back to him in detail, a particular pear tree that grew at a distance.

The first son, sent in winter, described the tree as "ugly, bent, and twisted." The second son, sent in early spring, said that it was "covered with green buds and was full of promise." The third son, sent in early summer, said that it was "laden with blossoms that smelled so sweet and looked so beautiful, it was the most graceful thing [he had] ever seen." The fourth son, sent at the harvest, said that it was "ripe and drooping with fruit, full of life and fulfillment."[6]

Despite the contradictory reports, each son was correct—at least in part. The discrepancies came from having seen *only one season* in the tree's life. The true picture of the tree required the compiled observations from *every* season.

In that same way, keep in mind that only God knows every detail about another's situation. You may be unaware of complex factors in an addict's life. You might not know about a traumatizing experience in the addict's past. While you should not condone the addict's behavior, be hesitant to pass judgment.

A related caution for those who care is that it is easy to get totally caught up in the problems of *another*. We may then lose perspective on our own primary challenge. No issue in another's life should distract us from dealing with our own growth issues. Step back and evaluate the situation. Have you become so consumed with the addict's problem that you are neglecting your life or family responsibilities? If so, it's time to return to God for balance and perspective and to those growth tasks in your life.

Beware, too, of offering help before the other person is ready to receive it. Most people pay lip service before they are serious about receiving help. The first time someone says "I need help" may only be rhetorical. Save your best shot until the person asking for help is coming to you wholeheartedly.

It is likely that the addict will be more sincere in asking for help after he has tried to change on his own and failed time and again. At this point the addict realizes he cannot overcome the addiction on his own. Also, if the addict's spouse or family has recently become aware of the problem, it is possible that the addict will seek help as a result of an ultimatum or strong insistence to enter treatment.

Finally, there is no foolproof way of knowing when the person is whole-hearted, but breaks from usual behavior are one indicator. For example, if the person had avoided eye contact during previous conversations about his need for help but is now willing to look you in the eye, that may be a positive sign.

Recovering from a pornography problem is primarily the responsibility of the person with the problem. Others may help, but the primary effort must come from the person afflicted. You cannot do this for someone else. It is all too easy for that person to say what others want to hear. Lip service accomplishes nothing—

except adding disappointment to the grief already felt.

Family, friends, and professionals sometimes find themselves working harder at the solution than the person with the problem. I suggest backing off and returning to prayer when this is the case. Confronting long-standing errors in thinking and behavior is a tedious process. When the person is truly ready and determined to change, the insights will click.

Frustration with those who refuse to get help, or with those who return to porn during or after treatment, has led many to conclude that the attraction to pornography cannot be overcome. It's true that there are great challenges in walking away from pornography. It takes determination and a willingness to accept help from God and others, but victory is possible. It requires the courage to look squarely into the deepest areas of fear and shame.

True freedom from pornography requires addressing the root causes. Many get discouraged when they learn that further digging is needed. In many respects,

---

꿔 꿔 꿔

Charlie came to treatment sessions for porn addiction right from work. He was covered from head to toe in grease spots. He worked long hours as a mechanic to support his wife and young son.

He was a good judge of character, and came to see his counselor as a straight shooter. Charlie would later state that he owed that counselor his life, because he realized that he was headed for certain destruction before they crossed

the "cure" runs counter to the expectations of our culture. Instead of quick answers and easy solutions, this process requires persistence over time. Instead of working in isolation, the typical healing process involves assistance from others. Spouses and other concerned family

---
ᄋ ᄋ ᄋ

paths. Unlike many of the others in his treatment group, Charlie continued to attend weekly sessions after he was permitted to report on an every-other-week basis. He offered his phone number to newcomers, and often spoke with them at length in the parking lot after sessions. The other men in the group came to respect Charlie, even though his pointed questions and frank rebukes sometimes caught them off guard.

members and friends supply the encouragement and support needed to keep
going when the going gets tough. Learning to trust others with the deepest issues
of life requires courage and boldness that
don't develop overnight.

Help Is Available

I am very grateful for each of you who
continue to read this book. You are not
alone. I know that on the surface it may
look like a lonely and frustrating journey.
But your connection to the one with the
porn problem presents an extraordinary
opportunity to play a part in profoundly
changing a life. Overcoming the pull of
pornography is really only the first part of
the life-changing drama. Intertwined in
the process of coming to moral purity are
new opportunities for the ones you care
about to discover their true identity and

walk more consistently in the purpose for which they were created. Wow! There is nothing more significant in life than that.

The next section will offer specific advice on what *you* can do to help someone say "No!" to pornography.

Part
Four

Taking the
Next Step

When there is a sudden loss of cabin pressure on a plane, passengers are instructed to first tend to their own oxygen needs before assisting others. The same principle applies when pornography use causes a sudden loss of security in a relationship. Family or friends may initially react in disbelief: "This can't be happening to me." Shock may then give way to self blame: "I thought I knew this person. How could I have missed the warning signs?" Eventually, anger becomes directed at the person using pornography. The intensity of this anger, which may be experienced in waves that come and go, can be frightening.

For some readers, the knowledge that a loved one is using pornography is a fresh wound. For others, the pain of this knowledge has been carried far too long. To all who are affected by another's use of pornography: *Self-care is the first order of business*. No, it isn't selfish to see that your needs are met first. You need to begin to heal from the trauma you have experienced, as well as equip yourself for difficult tasks that still lie ahead. Meeting the needs of others comes more easily for some than nurturing one's self.

Incorporate personal care into your daily life. Set aside time, even if it's just an hour during the week, that is just for you. You are likely to be surprised at how little it will take to help you feel somewhat better. *Where* do you feel most comfortable? Some may choose a spot in their home, while others may go for a walk or visit a special place. Choosing something simple and near at hand will maximize the benefit of this special time.

Take each of the five senses and consider what feels best to you. For example,

what would you like to *hear*? Options
may include soft music or just simple
silence. What *smells* do you prefer?
Choices may be a scented candle or
something baking. What would you like
to *touch*? Maybe a soft throw or a stuffed
animal. What would *taste* good right
now? Perhaps a specialty coffee or tea, a
crisp apple, or a treat. What would you
like to *see*? Looking at family photo-
graphs, a magazine, or reading a book
may be reminders that life goes on elsewhere. Many have found solace in reading
Scripture, particularly Psalms or a favorite
passage, or spending time in prayer.

Besides reserving a special time to
regroup and pray, try to eat healthy foods.
Exercise, drink water, and avoid alcohol.
Nap if you are able, and try to get to bed
a little earlier. Even if you can't sleep,
resting will help your body to rejuvenate.

Overcome the urge to withdraw and isolate. Find at least one other person with whom you can share the burdens of your heart. Be sure that person can keep a confidence. You may want to consider joining a support group or talking with a professional counselor.

Four Key Helpers

Remember that breaking free from the hold of pornography is primarily the work and responsibility of the person with the problem. But very few people overcome a pornography problem on their own. While there may be differences in the specific ways that people attain success, most who have done so acknowledge the contributions made by four key helpers:

- God
- A personal encourager

- A counselor
- An accountability partner

Understanding the role of each one may help you identify the part you can play in the life of someone struggling with pornography.

God

Even when He is not formally acknowledged, God takes a personal interest in every person and uses problems as opportunities to demonstrate His love and power. He wants people to experience freedom from pornography and prompts others to come alongside to help them.

God is the One who opens the human spirit to new understanding and motivates a person to pursue wholeness in every aspect of life. He alone knows the truth of one's past. The recovery process is like an archeological dig that begins with surface behaviors. Beneath those behaviors are emotions that are rooted in beliefs.

Personal Encourager

A personal encourager takes an ongoing personal interest in the one who struggles with pornography. Some personal encouragers work with, or are related to, the person with the pornography problem; others may be impressed to pray for someone they hardly know at all. Those who successfully overcome a pornography problem express gratitude for that "someone out there who believed in me" or "could see something of value in me." Personal encouragers often include parents, spouses, and others who must persuade a loved one to enter treatment.

Parents play a unique role in the company of personal encouragers, especially when dealing with a child in the home who may have a problem with porn. On the preventative level, they are entrusted with the responsibility of maintaining a healthy home environment in a temptation-filled culture. Keeping unhealthy influences out of the home is preferable to dealing with the consequences after that material has entered the home. Parents must effectively address the issue of the non-stop connection to the culture through television, videos, movies, and Internet access.

Families in which people have been successful in overcoming pornography report following a few basic rules. Parental controls and filter blocks are used to restrict access to porn through the Internet or cable TV. Televisions and computers are kept in plain view in common areas; this helps keep both children and parents accountable. The amount of time spent is closely monitored. If necessary, connecting cords are removed so that the equipment will not work after parents have gone to bed. The histories of Web sites accessed are checked regularly. The failure of one parent to properly protect children from objectionable material is no excuse for inaction by the other. Emphasizing the importance of self-control and instilling the value of making good moral choices are also two key factors in raising children with a healthy view of sexuality.

If pornography becomes an issue with minors in the home, parents, such as Lucy in the introduction, should evaluate the situation carefully and offer treatment options. The first level of intervention would be for Lucy to clearly explain God's purpose for sex, as well as her expectation for her son:

1. *Looking at sexual images is wrong.*
God wants sex to be special and personal
in marriage. I do not want pornography
in this home.

2. *I want you to come to me when you
have a problem.* I will help you find
answers. I do not want you to keep
secrets from me.

If she believes that her son understands
and will fully cooperate with her wishes,
careful monitoring and occasional accountability questions may be sufficient for him.
If she believes that he does not fully under-
stand, and/or is unwilling to honor her
expectations, she may arrange for a consultation with a counselor. Parents of minors
may insist on treatment, even if the minor
is reluctant or unwilling to participate.

Parents can best help adult children
who struggle with pornography through
prayer and encouragement. Offering

support rather than criticism will keep communication channels open. Encourage the adult child to make behavioral changes. For many, the depth of the problem and the dearth of personal resources will require professional assistance. Mastery over the attraction to pornography involves both knowledge and the consistent application of practical skills. If denial persists, parents may need to confront the addict. (See the section on Confrontation for more advice on this subject.)

Counselor

The counselor shows the person what is wrong with behaviors such as viewing pornography, and the steps necessary to correct these behaviors. The interaction may be face-to-face or through printed or video materials. Face-to-face interaction is usually most effective.

Some people may have incurred a recent interest in pornography and are willing and prepared to do whatever is necessary to change. For them, reading an Internet article or a book may be sufficient to begin a self-directed action plan. It is important to look for resources or programs that deal with the emotional and spiritual aspects of the problem, not only outward behavior.(See the Resources section for recommended materials.) Even reading a startling quote or statistic may trigger a new perspective.

For others who are trapped by the problem and cannot break the addiction on their own, talking with someone in a safe environment, such as meeting one-on-one with a counselor, can provide the opportunity for honest and open communication.

Because breaking free from pornography is generally not just a one-time decision, the majority of people benefit from the additional structure and ongoing contact provided in a formal coaching or counseling setting. Within the field of professional counseling, three common approaches are individual, group, and intensive counseling.

Individual counseling provides a confidential, one-on-one pairing with a pastor or counselor where personal issues may be systematically explored.

Group treatment may target those with the pornography problem or offer support to spouses and other family members. Group counseling provides the additional benefit of feedback from others who are dealing with similar issues. Some groups are limited to a specified number of weeks, while others may be ongoing.

Intensive counseling presents a focused approach where longer sessions are held on a daily basis, away from distractions.

Resources

BOOKS

Carder, Dave and Duncan Jaenicke. *Torn Asunder: Recovering from Extramarital Affairs*. Chicago: Moody Publishers, 1995.

Cloud, Dr. Henry and Dr. John Trent. *Boundaries in Marriage*. Grand Rapids, Mich.: Zondervan, 2002.

Condie, Joann. *Nothing to Hide: Hope for Marriages Hurt by Pornography and Infidelity*. Colorado Springs: Focus on the Family.

Dobson, Dr. James. *Love Must Be Tough: New Hope for Families in Crisis*. Sisters, Ore.: Multnomah Publishers, 2004.

Eggerichs, Dr. Emerson. *Love and Respect*. Franklin, Tenn.: Integrity Publishers, 2004.

Harley, Willard. *His Needs, Her Needs: Building an Affair-Proof Marriage*. Oxford, United Kingdom: Monarch Books, 1994.

Jenkins, Jerry. *Hedges: Loving Your Marriage Enough to Protect It*. Wheaton, Ill.: Crossway Books, 2005.

Roberts, Ted. *Pure Desire: Helping People Break Free from Sexual Struggles*. Ventura, Calif.: Regal Books, 1999.

Rosberg, Dr. Gary and Barbara Rosberg. *Healing the Hurt in Your Marriage*. Carol Stream, Ill.: Tyndale House Publishers, 2004.

Schaumburg, Harry. *False Intimacy: Understanding the Struggle of Sexual Addiction*. Colorado Springs: NavPress, 2000.

FOCUS ON THE FAMILY BROADCASTS

"Avoiding Infidelity I-II," Dr. Bob and Mrs. Cheryl Reccord, CT446 A-B.

"Overcoming Sexual Sin in Marriage," Mrs. Jennifer Ridgway, B00766D.

"Avoiding the Path to Moral Failure," Ted Haggard and H.B. London, CT317.

"Examining Addictive Behaviors I-II," Dr. Archibald Hart, CS587.

WEB SITES

www.pureintimacy.org
www.troubledwith.com

Dr. Bill Maier is Focus on the Family's vice president and psychologist in residence. Dr. Maier received his master's and doctoral degrees from the Rosemead School of Psychology at Biola University in La Mirada, California. A child and family psychologist, Dr. Maier hosts the national "Weekend Magazine" radio program and the "Family Minute with Dr. Bill Maier." He also acts as a media spokesperson for Focus on the Family on a variety of family-related issues. He and his wife, Lisa, have been married for more than seven years and have two children.

◗ ◗ ◗

Dr. Jim Vigorito is a licensed psychologist and has been listed on the National Register of Health Service Providers in Psychology since 1982. He is a Sex Offense-Specific Evaluator and Treatment Provider in Colorado. Dr. Vigorito served on the Psychology Augment Panel of the Colorado Mental Health Grievance Board from 1995 to 1998. He also served as an oral examiner for the Colorado Board of Psychologist Examiners. He has worked in the Counseling Department at Focus on the Family since 2000. Dr. Vigorito and his wife, Patricia, have been married for more than 20 years and have two grown children.

FOCUS ON THE FAMILY®

Welcome to the family!

Whether you purchased this book, borrowed it, or received it as a gift, we're glad you're reading it. It's just one of the many helpful, encouraging, and biblically based resources produced by Focus on the Family for people in all stages of life.

Focus began in 1977 with the vision of one man, Dr. James Dobson, a licensed psychologist and author of numerous best-selling books on marriage, parenting, and family. Alarmed by the societal, political, and economic pressures that were threatening the existence of the American family, Dr. Dobson founded Focus on the Family with one employee and a once-a-week radio broadcast aired on 36 stations.

Now an international organization reaching millions of people daily, Focus on the Family is dedicated to preserving values and strengthening and encouraging families through the life-changing message of Jesus Christ.

Focus on the Family Magazines

These faith-building, character-developing publications address the interests, issues, concerns, and challenges faced by every member of your family from preschool through the senior years.

| Focus on the Family **Citizen®** U.S. news issues | Focus on the Family **Clubhouse Jr.™** Ages 4 to 8 | Focus on the Family **Clubhouse™** Ages 8 to 12 | **Breakaway®** Teen guys | **Brio®** Teen girls 12 to 16 | **Brio & Beyond®** Teen girls 16 to 19 | **Plugged In®** Reviews movies, music, TV |

FOR MORE INFORMATION

Online:
Log on to www.family.org
In Canada, log on to
www.focusonthefamily.ca

Phone:
Call toll free: (800) A-FAMILY
In Canada, call toll free:
(800) 661-9800

Spouses may be invited to participate in
the intensive healing process.

Across these format options, choosing
counselors based on integrity and exper-
tise will increase the likelihood of a successful outcome. I recommend that the
pornography issue be dealt with before
engaging in other marital or family issues;
however, keep in mind that each situation
is unique. It is best to talk with a professional regarding which approach is best
for your specific situation.

Accountability Partner(s)

Accountability partners are others of the
same gender who meet at least weekly for
prayer and frank discussion. Some may
struggle with the same issues. Same-gender
relatives and coworkers serve especially
well as accountability partners because of
proximity. However, if the addict is too

embarrassed to discuss the problem with a family member or a coworker, he or she should find a partner through a place of worship or a support group.

Accountability partners help people process what they are learning in treatment outside of the counseling session. Accountability is the key to endurance. Recognizing how easy it is to deceive self and others, accountability partners should remain active for as long as possible. Rotating the specific accountability burden every six months to a year is one way of keeping these special helpers from burnout.

The hard questions must be asked with great regularity, the minimum being on a weekly basis. For example: *Have you engaged in any sexually explicit talk or material this week? Did you look at another with sexual intent in the past week? What did you do to enhance your relationship*

with your spouse or family? The final
question should always be something
similar to: *Have you been honest about
everything we have discussed?* The counseling department at Focus on the Family
maintains a more complete list of possible
accountability questions.

I do not recommend that a spouse or
a parent of the *opposite* gender (such as
Lucy) assume the accountability role.
Selecting a same-gender accountability
partner permits greater freedom in dis-
cussing details of sexual attractions and
the actions taken.

Spouses or pastors are often the first to
be proposed as accountability partners. It
is natural to consider them first because
they are close at hand and may already
know about the problem. However,
because of the personal pain caused by a
spouse's hesitation or failure to respond

properly to temptation, spouses should relinquish this role to others of the same gender as the porn user. And many pastors are too busy to consistently be available for this kind of accountability.

Sustaining Treatment

Recovery is generally not a straight line to the top. Most who struggle to overcome pornography have level spots, where forward progress is not evident, and even lapses and relapses. Personal encouragers and accountability partners stand in the gap for those who get discouraged. They maintain hope even when the person with the problem is discouraged and ready to give up. Many find this hope by looking to God. Balance an awareness of how difficult it is to face the most painful aspects of life with the importance of completing treatment.

The majority of sexually addicted men

I counsel are court-ordered to attend
sessions until treatment is completed.
Throughout the years, many other men
have joined the sessions on a volunteer
basis. Unfortunately, very few of these men
remained in treatment long enough to
ensure lasting results. They were prema-
ture in concluding that they had reached
the root of the problem, and no longer
wanted to invest the time and money necessary for total healing. Many who leave
treatment prematurely gradually let down
their guard and make moral compromises.

The three most important factors in
lasting change are:

- Radical honesty
- Self-imposed healthy boundaries
- Detailed accountability

Even under the best circumstances,
honesty tends to be progressive; that is,
the person with the problem will see and

report more as time goes on. Increased
confidence in reporting will be, at least in
part, a consequence of how past disclosures have been received.

Increasing attempts at honesty must
be encouraged. This is difficult when the
disclosures reflect a level of dysfunction
not previously imagined. Ideally, wrong
thinking and wrong behavior must be
addressed without personal condemnation. Many people with this problem
anticipate condemnation and rejection.
Like a wounded pet, they may strike out
at those providing care. Be prepared to
listen without being judgmental. Many
times this will be very difficult for you to
do. There may be instances when you
need to first take personal time to collect
your thoughts or pray for self-control and
then come together again to discuss the
problem.

Confrontation

How does a spouse or loved one convince
the person who is struggling that he or
she needs to get help? Efforts at persua-
sion are likely to be more successful when
the appeal is made on both *objective* and
relational grounds. For example, the earlier sections in this book present the
objective reality:

- Pornography use is wrong.
- Pornography hurts the family.
- Pornography should not be tolerated
  in the home.

The ideal proportion of affirmation to
confrontation is probably 5:1; that is, one
successful confrontation requires at least
five *prior* positive affirmations. People
become defensive, and may give up hope,
if they are hit with a barrage of all they
are doing wrong. Open the conversation
by listing the things that first attracted

you to the person or that you appreciate about him or her. Continue with the positive things the person has done over the years to build further trust and respect.

Your list of objective points should be limited to *two or three* of the most important things; any more than three points will be lost. Additional concerns must be addressed later.

The *relational* ground is introduced by telling the person how each behavior has affected the relationship. Do not make more than three points per behavior. Use "I feel . . ." statements. For example, after Sonia identifies her husband's looking at pornography as unacceptable, she might add: "*I felt betrayed* when you broke your wedding vow to me. *I felt rejected* when you preferred someone else to me. *I felt insecure* in my ability to interest and satisfy you."

Especially when confronting a male (who may be more likely to process information visually), it can be helpful to write things out and present them on paper. The written preparation can serve as talking points and then be given to the person to bring to mind the points that were discussed.

If the one-on-one approach is not successful, the need for help with a pornography problem should be brought to a third party in the hope of resolution. If the person belongs to a church, approach the pastor or designated authority. If the person is not affiliated with a church, arrange to speak with a respected family member or friend.

Respectfully inform the person with the pornography problem that in an effort to seek resolution, you have arranged to meet with a third party. Ask the porn user to participate and make it clear that you will keep the appointment even if he chooses not to do so.

Adopt the attitude that you are standing alongside to help the person. Remem-

—————— ୨ ୨ ୨ ——————

In our 24 years of marriage, my wife has written me two confrontational letters. I hadn't really heard her when she made previous attempts at conversation. She was careful to begin each letter by affirming her love, assuming my cooperation, and acknowledging areas in which I had done well. She then put forth the areas of her concern, asking that I get back to her with an answer. I recognized what she was saying only after she put the concerns of her heart onto paper. Once I understood her concerns, I made the changes she requested.

ber that the objective is behavioral change and healing. It is crucial to separate the *behavior* from the *person*; addressing the wrong behavior is different from criticizing the person.

Some prefer to enlist the services of a professional counselor to provide third-party authority. One advantage of this approach is that issues can be addressed apart from ongoing relationships at church and in the family. A second advantage is that the counselor may be more readily available than a pastor or family member for ongoing follow-up. Whenever possible, seek assistance from counselors who specialize in helping people with pornography addictions.

Countering Resistance

Expect strong resistance to early efforts at change. Pornography problems undercut a person's effectiveness inside and outside the home. Changing long-standing behavioral patterns is difficult.

A common complaint is that "it shouldn't have to be so hard." Sorry, folks, but it is hard. Patterns of sexual arousal are among the most difficult things to change. People who have overcome addiction to alcohol and drugs report that overcoming their sexual addiction was more difficult. I believe that one of the reasons for this is that it is easier to avoid alcohol and drugs than it is to avoid sexual memories or images. Also, the smell of alcohol or the behavioral consequences of substance abuse are more easily identified than the consequences of sexual relapse; therefore the user can be more quickly and easily called to accountability.

Families also grow weary of the ongoing investment of time and energy. Some family members fear confronting their loved one or reporting their concerns to treatment providers or accountability members. Typically, these individuals will come to regret overlooking these lapses. Peace in the short term will result in further lapses.

Also, by ignoring the problem or choosing to overlook questionable behavior, family members and friends enable the addict to continue in his or her unhealthy behavior. The denial that was prevalent before treatment began will return with a vengeance, this time bolstered by a perverted validation that the problem with pornography isn't really a big deal after all. These individuals may become resistant to future treatment, concluding that they tried it once and were unsuccessful. The slide back down is always quicker than the slow trek up.

It May Be Necessary to Separate

Despite the efforts of others, some people refuse to get help for a pornography problem. They may insist on bringing objectionable material into the home, or crossing the line into more deviant behaviors. Many spouses wonder where to draw the line between what is accommodated and what is not.

Clearly, some behaviors must not be tolerated. For example, physically forcing a spouse into unwanted sex (rape) is against the law. Beyond criminal violations in the home, the person with a pornography problem may engage in sex outside the home. Extramarital sex poses a serious health risk to the spouse. Sexual relations in the marriage should not be resumed until testing and treatment for venereal diseases are completed.

A time of separation may be necessary

for the offender to fully realize the wrong-
fulness of the behavior. Seek advice from
a trained counselor in these situations. A
third-party intervention can provide an
objective perspective.

But what about emotional abuse?
Should a spouse stay in the home if the
addict refuses to seek treatment? Dr.
James Dobson, founder of Focus on the
Family and a licensed psychologist, talks
about the need for tough love in marriages, the idea being that a passive
approach will often lead to dissolution
of the relationship.[7]

As a spouse, relative, or close friend,
you have the right and the responsibility
(especially in the case of a spouse or parent) to hold the addict accountable for
his behavior. While you may not be his or
her accountability partner, you *can* expect
the addict to make a consistent effort to

change his or her unhealthy behavior. If the addict consistently disrespects his partner and/or children by continuing to view pornography, it may be necessary to separate in order to force the addict to choose between the comfort of living at home with his family or living with his addiction.

Any kind of sexual interaction between adults and minors is also against the law. A violation of this nature should be immediately reported to either law enforcement or social services. Until granted permission by legal authorities, offenders are generally not permitted to live with, or even have contact with, victims or minors. For the nonoffending parent, failure to adequately protect minors from sexual harm may be grounds for removal of the children from the home. It is the responsibility of parents to protect their children and to provide a loving and safe environment for them, no matter how embarrassing it may be to make the problem "public."

Remember that different situations will require different solutions. It is best to contact a professional counselor in order to receive appropriate advice for your situation.

Protection from Pornography: Living the Alternative

I think the final challenge for the addict in overcoming a pornography problem is realizing that life will *never* return to the way things were. The old way of life must die and be buried, never to be dug up again. The person with the problem, as well as others affected by it, may fear that there will be nothing left after the problem is gone.

But what is really buried is the lie that satisfaction can be found through pornography. The deeper lesson learned in overcoming a pornography problem is recognizing one's weakness and realizing that the problem cannot be solved without help. The first step for the person struggling is to admit the problem. This begins the long road to recovery.

What can you do to help during this process? Celebrate the anniversaries of milestones on the path to making right choices. For example, three months into treatment, give the addict a personal card of encouragement for his or her effort. Prepare a special dinner or have an evening out to celebrate every year that the addict has been free from pornography. Because this struggle will likely be a long-term battle against addiction, reminding the addict that he is loved and supported reinforces why he is getting help.

Offer encouragement to others who are just beginning the process of discovery. This is an excellent way to review the basic steps of restoration. Speak honestly to your loved one or friend when he or she needs to hear truth. But remember to speak the truth *in love*. Offer your prayer support. And remember to pay attention to your personal needs. Take time for yourself.

A final word is in order pertaining to lapses. Many porn addicts will fail to heed the warning signs and slip back into wrong behavior patterns. When this occurs, instead of sinking into despair, it is time to knock the dust from the knees and start walking right again.

Realizing that God is still in control

may free you from carrying an unneces-
sary burden. Your primary role will be to
put the matter in God's hands—again and
again. Your loved one may hear the truth
more easily from another. Pray for God to
bring someone with a positive influence
into his or her life.

Because porn addiction is rooted in
deep issues, healing is likely to be a long
process. And this book has only scratched
the surface. For more help, contact Focus
on the Family for resources or to speak
with a counselor. Focus on the Family's
counseling department takes calls at 719-
531-3400, extension 7700, between the
hours of 9 A.M. and 4:30 P.M., Mountain
Time, Monday through Friday. You can
receive referrals for counselors in your
area who specialize in addressing these
issues from a biblical perspective. There

are also centers that specialize in intensive counseling for sexual issues for periods ranging from four to 10 days or longer.

When necessary, Focus's licensed counselors are available for a brief one-time consultation. The counselors may suggest resources pertinent to your specific circumstances. A list of relevant materials is also provided in the Resources section at the back of the book.

I hope that this book has encouraged you as you share in the struggle of one caught up in pornography. I pray that you and your loved one will work together to rebuild the life that has been broken. Do not give up the struggle until each of the underlying misconceptions and deceptions is uncovered and healing has taken place.

Above all, I pray that you will personally experience God's great patience and loving concern for you, and that your loved one will find healing.

Notes

1. "Pornified America—The Culture of Pornography," August 22, 2005, http://www.albert mohler.com/commentary_read.php?cdate=20 05-08-022 (accessed June 2, 2006).
2. Ibid.
3. Jerry Ropelato, "Internet Pornography Statistics," TopTenREVIEWS, Inc., http://internet-filter-review.toptenreviews.com/internet-porn ography-statistics.html (accessed April 27, 2006).
4. Archibald Hart, *Examining Addictive Behaviors I-II*, Focus on the Family Daily Broadcast (CS 587A-B).
5. Matthew 7:1-5.
6. Author Unknown, *Lessons on Life*, http:// www.mil.ufl.edu/3701/pear_tree.html (accessed May 12, 2006).
7. Dr. James C. Dobson, *Love Must Be Tough* (Nashville, TN: Word Publishing, 1996), 57.

More Great Resources
from Focus on the Family®